A GUIDED TOUR THROUGH HISTORY

Antietam

HELP US KEEP THIS GUIDE UP TO DATE

We would love to hear from you concerning your experiences with this guide and how you feel it could be improved and kept up to date. Please send your comments and suggestions to:

editorial@GlobePequot.com

Thanks for your input, and happy travels!

A Timeline Book

A GUIDED TOUR THROUGH HISTORY

Antietam

CYNTHIA PARZYCH

With an introduction by James C. Bradford

travel

Guilford, Connecticut

An imprint of The Globe Pequot Press

Project editor: Lynn Zelem
Maps: Trailhead Graphics © Morris Book Publishing, LLC
Historical PopOut map and historical interior maps on pp. vi, 21, and 58 courtesy of the Library of Congress.

All photos courtesy of the Library of Congress, except for the following: Photos on pp. v, 22 (bottom), 27, 35, 42, and 47 by C. Parzych; photos on pp. 33, 55, 76, 78, and 79 courtesy of the National Park Service; photo on p. 36 courtesy of National Park Service, Keith Snyder, photographer; photo on p. 6 from Shutterstock; photos on pp. 23, 38, and 60 from Shutterstock © Kurt Holter; photo on p. 54 from Shutterstock © Pete Hoffman; photos on pp. 80 and 82 courtesy of Bavarian Inn; photo on p. 81 courtesy of Stone Manor.

Library of Congress Cataloging-in-Publication Data is available on file.
ISBN 978-0-7627-5328-4

Printed in China
10 9 8 7 6 5 4 3 2 1

All the information in this guidebook is subject to change. We recommend that you call ahead to obtain current information before traveling. All restaurants are open daily for breakfast, lunch, and dinner, unless otherwise noted.

Contents

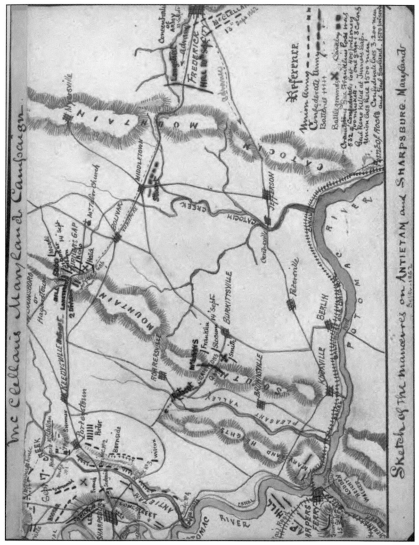

A contemporary sketch of the Maryland Campaign.

Introduction

by JAMES C. BRADFORD

On September 17, 1862, the Confederate Army of Northern Virginia and the U.S. Army of the Potomac met at Antietam in the bloodiest single day's fighting in American history. A year and a half had passed since eleven Southern states had reacted to the election of Abraham Lincoln by seceding from the Union and forming the Confederate States of America. Southern secessionists feared that the ascent to power of Lincoln and his fellow Republicans threatened their way of life. Many of them unrealistically hoped for a peaceful division of the nation, but in April 1861 the new president called for 75,000 volunteers to crush the rebellion and save the Union. For over a year Confederate leaders pursued a defensive strategy, but as the prospect for a negotiated peace disappeared, Confederate commander Robert E. Lee shifted to the offensive hoping to force a settlement, but the plan backfired when his advance into Maryland was stopped at Sharpsburg near Antietam Creek, 70 miles northwest of Washington, D.C.

The Battle of Antietam, or Sharpsburg, as Southerners refer to it, marked a turning point in the war. It ended the first Confederate invasion of Union territory, secured the U.S. capital at Washington from danger for almost a year, and reinvigorated Union morale.

The Setting

The first year of the Civil War was far from conclusive. Neither side was adequately prepared when their armies met at Bull Run, near Manassas, Virginia, in July 1861. Indeed, command, control, and discipline were so primitive in the initial large-scale encounter between the Union and Confederate armies that neither commander, Brigadier General Irvin McDowell of the Army of the Potomac nor his Southern counterpart, Brigadier General P. G. T. Beauregard, could fully execute his plans or take advantage of tactical opportunities that developed. Casualties were relatively light compared to later battles, but the engagement dispelled illusions in both the North and South that victory could be won easily or quickly. Both armies retired to lick their wounds and reorganize. Assuming command of the Army of the Potomac on July 27, Major

General George B. McClellan devoted the remainder of 1861 to equipping and training its units.

Abandoning any idea of an offensive in northern Virginia, the Union launched a series of attacks against positions along the Atlantic coast of the Confederacy that resulted in the capture and occupation of Fort Hatteras, North Carolina, on August 28, 1861, and Port Royal, South Carolina, on November 7. Meanwhile, in the west, Confederate forces defeated Union troops at Wilson's Creek, Missouri, the first major engagement west of the Allegheny Mountains, on August 10.

The new year of 1862 opened with a series of Union victories in the west when a naval flotilla commanded by Flag Officer Andrew Foote hammered Fort Henry on the Tennessee River into surrender (February 6), followed by the surrender of Fort Donelson on the Cumberland River to troops commanded by Major General Ulysses S. Grant (February 16), and the occupation of Nashville (February 25) by troops led by Brigadier General Don Carlos Buell. Capture of the forts and city, the first major Confederate city taken by Union troops, brought much of the state of Tennessee under the control of Federal forces. Further west a U.S. army commanded by Brigadier General Samuel Curtis repulsed an attack by Confederate forces on his position at Pea Ridge in northwestern Arkansas (March 7–8). Meanwhile another Union army, this one commanded by Brigadier General John Pope and supported by Andrew Foote's gunboat, laid siege to Island No. 10 in the Mississippi River (beginning on February 28), forcing its surrender (April 8). Union operations were not as successful to the southeast, where Major General Ulysses S. Grant's drive south from Forts Henry and Donelson was stopped at Shiloh near Pittsburg Landing (April 6) by Confederate forces commanded by Gen-

CIVIL WAR TIMELINE	1860		1861		
	November 6 Abraham Lincoln elected president.	**December 20** South Carolina secedes from the Union. Mississippi, Alabama, Florida, Georgia, Louisiana, and Texas follow within two months.	**February 9** Confederate States of America (C.S.A.) forms; Jefferson Davis is president.	**March 4** Lincoln inaugurated as president of the United States.	**April 12** Fort Sumter is bombarded by Confederate army.
					April 17 Virginia secedes; Arkansas, Tennessee, and North Carolina follow.
					April 20 Robert E. Lee resigns his commission in the U.S. Army.

eral Albert Sidney Johnston and forced to withdraw. Later that month Union navy ships commanded by Flag Officer David G. Farragut ran past Forts Jackson and St. Phillip on the lower Mississippi and proceeded 70 miles upriver to New Orleans, where Federal troops occupied the city without firing a shot (April 24). Thus Union forces seemed to be making progress in the west in early 1862.

The Approach to Antietam

Such was not the case in the Virginia theater of operations. After months of preparations Major General George B. McClellan launched the Peninsula Campaign in March 1862. Using 389 vessels, he moved the 146,000-man Army of the Potomac by water from Alexandria, Virginia, and Annapolis, Maryland, to Fort Monroe, on the tip of the peninsula formed by the York and James Rivers. McClellan hoped to outflank Confederate defenses in northern Virginia and to attack the Confederate capital at Richmond from the south-east. Major General John B. Magruder's 13,000 Confederates dashed Yankee hopes of a quick victory when they checked the advance of McClellan's army at a series of earthworks they hastily erected across the peninsula. General Joseph E. Johnston soon arrived to take overall command of Confederate forces in the inconclusive Battle of Fair Oaks/Seven Pines (May 31), during which Johnston was wounded. Robert E. Lee took command of Confederate forces and launched a series of offenses, the Seven Days Battles (June 25–July 1, 1862), that led McClellan to retreat and President Abraham Lincoln to order the Army of the Potomac back to Washington.

 With Richmond safe from the southeast, Lee rushed forces to fend off

1862

July 21	**November 1**	**January 31**	**February 6**	**April 6–7**
Battle of Bull Run (First Manassas)	President Lincoln appoints George B. McClellan general-in-chief of the U.S. Army.	Lincoln issues General War Order No. 1, calling for U.S. forces to advance by February 22.	Major General Ulysses S. Grant captures Fort Henry in Tennessee, and Fort Donelson ten days later.	Confederates surprise Grant at Shiloh; 23,000 men are killed or wounded in the fighting.
				April 24 Flag Officer David Farragut leads seventeen Union ships to occupy New Orleans.

Union troops observe Lee's army crossing the Potomac at White's Ford.

an attack from the north by the Army of Virginia, led by Major General John Pope. A series of brilliant tactical moves by Lee culminated in the Second Battle of Manassas (August 28–30, 1862), a defeat so complete that the Army of Virginia was disbanded and its forces transferred to the Army of the Potomac.

Confederate commander Robert E. Lee immediately realized the opportunity open to him and decided to swing west of Washington, D.C., cross the

1862

May 31
Battle of Seven Pines: Confederate General Joseph Johnston attacks near Richmond; the battle is inconclusive.

June 1
General Robert E. Lee replaces General Joseph Johnston and assumes command of the Army of Northern Virginia.

June 25–July 1
The Seven Days Battles near Richmond; McClellan begins withdrawal from the South.

July 11
General Henry Halleck becomes general-in-chief of the U.S. Army.

August 28–30
Second Manassas: Generals James Longstreet and Stonewall Jackson defeat the Union Army of the Potomac.

September 2–5
General McClellan placed in command and leads the Union army out of Washington, D.C., at the beginning of the Maryland Campaign.

September 4
General Lee crosses the Potomac with his army and proceeds to Frederick, Maryland.

September 10
Confederates approach Boonsboro, Hagerstown, and Maryland Heights.

September 12
Union troops arrive in Frederick.

Harpers Ferry, 1861.

Potomac River, and strike northward toward Harrisburg, the capital of Pennsylvania. By forcing the Union army to follow him, he prevented its invading the South and disrupting the harvest season. Lee anticipated that once his army was in Maryland, men from that slave state would rally to the Southern cause and join his army. He also believed that a defeat of the Army of the Potomac in Union territory might well empower supporters of the Confederacy in Europe and influence voters in the congressional elections scheduled by Northern states for the fall of that year.

September 13
McClellan is handed a copy of Lee's Special Order 191 indicating Lee's plans of operation.

September 14
Battle of South Mountain and the siege of Harpers Ferry.

September 15
Harpers Ferry surrenders to the Confederates; Lee's army ordered to concentrate at Sharpsburg.

September 16
Union forces led by General Hooker cross Antietam Creek and engage the Confederate left that afternoon.

September 17
Battle of Antietam fought at Sharpsburg: 26,000 men are dead or wounded by day's end and battle is a draw.

September 18
Lee's army crosses the Potomac that evening, withdrawing to Virginia.

September 20
Battle of Shepherdstown.

September 22
Lincoln issues a preliminary Emancipation Proclamation.

October 1–4
Lincoln comes to Sharpsburg to meet with Union troops.

November 7
Lincoln replaces McClellan with Major General Ambrose Burnside.

December 13
Burnside is roundly defeated at Fredericksburg.

View of Harpers Ferry from the Maryland side.

On September 3 Lee ordered his men to break camp at Chantilly, Virginia, and to head northwestward to cross the Potomac at White's Ford near Leesburg (September 4–7), and to make camp at Frederick, Maryland. Pausing there, Lee received reports from cavalry sent to reconnoiter the enemy. Learning that 12,000 Yankee troops remained garrisoned in Harpers Ferry, 20 miles to the west, in a position from which they might sever his lines of communication with Virginia, Lee divided his forces, sending the majority with General Thomas "Stonewall" Jackson to capture or disperse the Federal

1863

January 1
Lincoln issues the formal Emancipation Proclamation, freeing all slaves in Confederate territories.

January 25
Lincoln replaces Burnside with Major General Joseph Hooker.

May 1-4
Lee defeats Hooker at Chancellorsville; Stonewall Jackson is wounded and dies on May 10.

June 3
Lee begins his march to the North, entering Pennsylvania with 75,000 soldiers.

June 28
Lincoln replaces Hooker with Major General George Meade.

July 1–3
Meade defeats Lee at Gettysburg, turning the tide of the war.

July 4
A six-week siege at Vicksburg ends with Confederate surrender to Grant.

September 19–20
The Union Army of the Cumberland becomes trapped in Chattanooga, Tennessee, when it is defeated at Chickamauga.

garrison there. On September 10 Brigadier General John Walker led his men southward out of Frederick to occupy Loudoun Heights, south of Harpers Ferry; Major General Lafayette McLaws and Major General Richard Heron Anderson passed through Crampton's Gap in South Mountain to approach Harpers Ferry at Maryland Heights; and Stonewall Jackson led three divisions through Turner's Gap to cross the Potomac at Williamsport and approach Harpers Ferry from Martinsburg, Virginia. Lee hoped to use South Mountain, a 1,300-foot-high extension of the Blue Ridge Mountains, to mask these movements and those of the remainder of his army, which he and General James Longstreet marched northwestward through Boonsboro toward Hagerstown.

Learning that Lee had left his position at Chantilly, McClellan marched in pursuit on September 5. When the Army of the Potomac arrived at the abandoned Confederate campground in Frederick (September 12), an observant Union corporal found a copy of Lee's Special Order No. 191, detailing the division of his army, wrapped around three cigars and lying on the ground. Seeing an opportunity to position his unified army between the two portions of the Confederate army, McClellan sent cavalry westward to see if Turner's Gap was held by Confederate forces and ordered Major General William Franklin and his Sixth Corps to pass through Crampton's Gap to reinforce Harpers Ferry. Informed by an agent that McClellan had a copy of Lee's plans and was moving toward him, Major General Daniel Harvey Hill sent the agent on to Lee's headquarters then returned to Turner's Gap with 2,300 of his men. Lee reacted to the news by ordering Hill to hold Turner's Gap and Fox's Gap a mile to the south, as long as possible, and sent Longstreet with the majority of his corps back to South Mountain with orders to check the

		1864			
October 16 Lincoln appoints Grant commander of the West.	**November 19** Soldiers National Cemetery is dedicated at Gettysburg; Lincoln gives the Gettysburg Address.		**March 9** Lincoln appoints Grant as general-in-chief.	**May 5–6 and 8–12** Battles in Wilderness and Spotsylvania turn the war in the Union's favor; Major General William Sherman begins a march to Atlanta with 100,000 men.	**June 15** The nine-month Union siege of Petersburg begins.
	November 23–25 The Union army finally defeats the Confederates under General Braxton Bragg at Chattanooga.				

Battle of South Mountain.

Union advance long enough for Jackson to recall his army from Harpers Ferry and reunite with the rest of the Army of Northern Virginia.

The Battle of South Mountain began when Federal cavalry, commanded by Brigadier General Alfred Pleasanton, struck Hill's position at Turner's Gap early on September 14, 1862. Brigadier General Jacob D. Cox soon arrived with his division to support the attack, followed by Major General Joseph Hooker with the First Corps. Three hours later the Union Ninth Corps, commanded by Major General Jesse L. Reno, struck at Confederates holding Fox's Gap. Another 4½ miles to the south, Franklin and the U.S. Army's Sixth

1864

September 2
Sherman captures Atlanta.

November 8
Lincoln is reelected president.

November 15
Sherman begins the March to the Sea.

December 5–16
55,000 Union troops defeat Major General John Hood's army at Nashville.

December 21
Sherman reaches Savannah and the sea, leaving a swath of destruction in his wake.

Corps engaged Major General Lafayette McLaws's Confederates at Crampton's Gap. Lee arrived in the mid-afternoon and took command of Confederate defenses. By then 28,480 Union soldiers were in action against 17,852 Confederates, who fought tenaciously until forced to give way at 10:00 p.m. In what became known as the Battle of South Mountain, the number of Union troops killed or wounded was slightly greater than that for the Confederates. Each side had fewer than 500 killed, but more than 1,500 wounded. The number of men missing in action is difficult to calculate, but Confederate losses were clearly greater than those suffered by the Union.

As Hill and Longstreet withdrew toward Sharpsburg that night and early on the morning of September 15, Lee began establishing his defensive perimeter north and west of the town.

Aftermath of Antietam

As Lee began withdrawing southward toward the Potomac at dark on September 18, his hopes for a campaign that would alter the course of the war crushed, McClellan was quick to claim victory, but slow to pursue his foe to bring to an end the first invasion of the North by Confederate troops. Losses at Antietam were horrifying:

	Union	Confederate	Total
Killed	2,100	1,550	3,650
Wounded	9,550	7,750	17,300
Captured or Missing	750	1,020	1,770
TOTAL	12,400	10,320	22,720

1865

January 31	March 25	April 2	May
The Thirteenth Amendment officially abolishes slavery.	Lee's forces in Petersburg attack Grant's army, and are defeated in four hours.	Lee evacuates Petersburg. Richmond is evacuated.	The C.S.A. reunites with the United States.

April 9
Lee surrenders to Grant at Appomattox.

April 14
John Wilkes Booth shoots Lincoln at Ford's Theatre in Washington. Lincoln dies the next morning at 7:22 a.m.

April 18
General Johnston surrenders to Sherman in North Carolina.

Lincoln with McClellan at Sharpsburg, October 1862.

Four days after the bloodiest single day of combat in U.S. history drew to a close, President Abraham Lincoln issued the preliminary Emancipation Proclamation to take effect on January 1, 1863. Together the victory at Antietam and the Emancipation Proclamation marked a turning point in the Civil War. The outcome of the battle raised Northern morale and was a setback for the Confederates in Europe, where their diplomats had hoped that a successful campaign in Union territory would lead to British and French recognition of the Confederate States of America and perhaps even their sending of warships to counter the Union blockade. The Emancipation Proclamation instilled new spirit in the Northern cause, adding a crusade against slavery to its struggle to save the Union. It was also a key step in the direction of mobilizing additional manpower for Union armies because Lincoln followed up by authorizing the formation of the first black regiments in the Union army.

On October 2 the president visited the battlefield to confer with McClellan in person and prod him into action. When the general continued to tarry, Lincoln issued direct orders to him to "cross the Potomac and give battle to the enemy or drive him south" (October 6). McClellan continued to procrastinate, so exasperating Lincoln that he finally fired the general, and Major General Ambrose Burnside assumed command of the Army of the Potomac on November 7.

This Hallowed Ground

Several hospitals were established to care for the wounded in the aftermath of battle, and the dead were buried in makeshift graves. In 1865 the Maryland legislature purchased 11.25 acres for a cemetery, and during the following two years donations from individuals from eighteen states made possible the purchase of additional land. On September 17, 1867, President Andrew Johnson spoke at the dedication of the Antietam National Cemetery. By then the work of moving bodies to the site was nearly completed with the interment of 4,776 Union soldiers, 1,836 of them of unknown identity. On March

Graves at Antietam National Cemetery.

13, 1878, Maryland deeded ownership of the cemetery to the federal government, which has operated it since. Another 255 veterans were buried in the cemetery before it was declared closed in 1953. An exception was made, however, to allow the internment of a victim of the 2000 terrorist attack on the USS *Cole* who was a resident of nearby Keedysville, Maryland.

In 1880 the first official government monument was erected on the battlefield to commemorate those who died during the Antietam Campaign. A massive 250-ton statue of a private soldier, it stood at the entrance to the Centennial Exposition in Philadelphia during 1876. It was then disassembled and moved to Sharpsburg, where it was formally dedicated on September 17, the eighteenth anniversary of the battle. A decade later (August 30, 1890) the Antietam National Battlefield Site was established by the War Department, whose preservation of the battlefield made it one of the most popular sites for veteran reunions. On August 10, 1933, the park was transferred to the National Park Service of the Department of Interior. Redesignated the Antietam National Battlefield on November 10, 1978, the grounds encompass 3,256 acres that include virtually the entire battlefield. All landscape features have been preserved or re-created except the East and West Woods, which are smaller than in 1862, but they are being expanded as new trees are planted. Combined with the compact size of the battlefield, this makes the Battle of Antietam one of the easiest for modern visitors to visualize.

Key Participants

Officers of the Confederacy

Brigadier General Ambrose Powell "A. P." Hill

A professional soldier born in Culpepper, Virginia, and educated at West Point (1847), Ambrose Hill and his Light Division saved the day for the Confederacy at Antietam. Having stayed behind to organize the captured Union forces and to remove property taken at Harpers Ferry, Hill commanded the last Confederate division to arrive during the battle at Antietam. Hill's timing, after a seven-hour, 17-mile forced march to Sharpsburg, when his troops seemed just to appear out of clouds of dust on the horizon, threw chaos into the Union divisions, just as they were threatening to flatten Lee's weakened right flank. Hill's troops broke the Union charge, and after more fighting, the battle ended.

Major General Daniel Harvey "D. H." Hill
The brother-in-law of Stonewall Jackson, Daniel Hill, born in South Carolina, was a mathematics scholar with a strong religious belief. He attended West Point and graduated in 1842. After the Civil War he became a magazine publisher and resumed an academic career. Hill earned a reputation as an aggressive and capable military man, as the hard fighting he led at the Battle of South Mountain demonstrated. At Antietam he had three horses shot out from under him and was a key participant in the horrific fighting in the Bloody Lane. His dry, sarcastic humor and disagreements with General Robert E. Lee, among others, probably contributed to his military skills being underutilized as the Civil War continued.

Brigadier General John Bell Hood The youngest man to earn the rank of full general in the Confederate army, John Hood was a leader who inspired the love of his troops. Born in Kentucky, he had attended West Point (1853) and when his home state did not secede from the Union, he resigned his commission in the U.S. Army in April 1861 to serve with the Fourth Texas Cavalry. Under his command the men of the Texas Brigade, the only western brigade to fight with the Army of Northern Virginia, earned a reputation as excellent shock troops. He was thirty-one years old at the time of the Antietam battle and one of Lee's most effective and respected generals. Eighty-two percent of his regiment was killed, lost, or wounded in forty-five minutes of hand-to-hand fighting in Miller's Cornfield. He lost the use of his left arm after being wounded at Gettysburg.

General Thomas "Stonewall" Jackson West Virginia–born Thomas Jackson graduated from West Point in 1846. His fearless, aggressive fighting, always intelligently executed, earned Jackson, as well as his brigade, their famous moniker at First Bull Run, where he and his men stood up to a Union attack "like a stone wall." After capturing Harpers Ferry, Jackson raced to Sharpsburg, where he was in the thick of the fighting at Antietam, but nonetheless feeding Lee tactical advice throughout that bloody day. General Lee had only the highest regard for Jackson, who was idolized by his soldiers. When he lost his arm at Chancellorsville (he died eight days later), General Lee wrote to him, "You have lost your left. I have lost my right arm."

General Robert E. Lee The most famous of Confederate generals, Robert E. Lee was a highly intelligent, polished man, beloved by his troops, with an aggressive military approach to war. After graduating West Point (1829) he rose to the rank of lieutenant colonel of the Second Cavalry in 1857 and was serving in Texas at the time of the secession crisis when General Winfield Scott recalled Lee to Washington and offered him command of the U.S. Army. Lee considered it but resigned from the army to support his home state of Virginia. Eight days after it seceded, Lee became commander of Virginia's forces. On June 1 Lee became commander of the Army of Northern Virginia, after General Joe Johnston was wounded in the spring of 1862. At Antietam his army was about half the size of McClellan's. Nonetheless, he managed to maneuver his brave and capable forces with precision into the right position each and every time it became necessary during the long and bloody day. Lee's critics feel he took too many chances at Sharpsburg, but no one can deny, despite the outcome and the ultimate withdrawal of the Confederate army into Virginia, who the better general was that day.

Major General James Longstreet Born in South Carolina and West Point–educated (1842), James Longstreet was one of the great generals of the Civil War. After serving in the Mexican-American War with distinction and resigning from the U.S.

Army in 1861, Longstreet went on to command a Confederate brigade. Troops who served under him called him "Old Pete" because of his tough, rocklike character and coolness in battle. Serving as corps commander under General Lee for most of the Army of Northern Virginia's best-known battles, Lee called Longstreet his "Old War Horse." At Antietam Longstreet was a key figure in holding the Confederate left in the most vicious fighting of the entire day's battle. Because of a chafed heel, he was forced to wear a carpet slipper throughout the days' events. His staff officer, Moxley Sorrel, wrote, "At Sharpsburg he was in no good humor at such footwear. . . . In fact, a wobbly carpet slipper was not a good-looking thing for a commander in the field."

Major General James E. B. Stuart Commissioned into the cavalry after graduating from the U.S. Military Academy (1854), James E. B. Stewart assisted Robert E. Lee during John Brown's raid on Harpers Ferry in 1859. Virginia-born Stuart resigned from the U.S. Army in 1861 and took the rank of colonel with the First Virginia Cavalry. An audacious military man, his scouting and harassment skills were invaluable to General Lee. He also had a reputation as a show-off and a ladies' man. At Antietam he held the key position of guarding the Confederate left wing in Lee's overall strategy. In Lee's mind Stuart was the "eyes and ears" of the entire Maryland campaign.

Officers of the Union

Major General Ambrose E. Burnside Best remembered for his distinctive whiskers and side-burns, Ambrose Burnside was born in Indiana and educated at West Point (1847). His early military career showed great promise. His leadership in the capture of Fort Macon from the Confederates in April 1862 made him a national hero, a reputation that was badly eroded after the hesitation he showed at Antietam. Taking most of the day to take the Lower Bridge on Antietam Creek, the delays and poor management he demonstrated allowed the Confederates, with the sudden arrival of A. P. Hill's brigade from Harpers Ferry, to hold off the final Union attempt to take Sharpsburg and potentially finally stop Lee's army.

Brigadier General George S. Greene Considered one of the most aggressive and resourceful commanders in the army, George Greene was born in Rhode Island, graduated from West Point in 1823, and served in the military for twelve years, leaving to become a civil engineer. At age sixty when the Civil War broke out, Greene left his lucrative business to become colonel of the Sixtieth New York Infantry Regiment, serving for the entire war. Commanding part of the Twelfth Corps at Antietam, his tenacity during the toughest morning fighting of the battle saw him taking the high ground in front of the Dunker Church and holding it with too few men and little ammunition, then breeching the Confederate left behind the church—the deepest penetration of any Union force that day.

Having taken too many losses after a four-hour fight, Greene had to withdraw. Demonstrating his toughness and good sensibility in holding Culp's Hill, Greene distinguished himself again at Gettysburg. Lieutenant George K. Collins, who served under Greene, said of him, "He knew how to drill, how to command, and in the hour of peril how to care for his command, and the men respected him accordingly."

Major General Joseph "Fighting Joe" Hooker
Commander of First Corps of the Army of the Potomac, Joseph Hooker was born in Hadley, Massachusetts, went to West Point (1837), served in Florida and Mexico, left the army in 1853, and rejoined the army at the beginning of the Civil War. Hooker earned himself a reputation as an aggressive military leader who focused on the key points in a battle. He was always keenly interested in the morale and welfare of his men. This was a general who led from the front, setting an example for his men, who respected and admired him. Hooker led the Union First Corps through some of the bloodiest action in the opening hours of Antietam against Stonewall Jackson's division. Just as Hooker could see a breakthrough in the long morning's well-matched fighting near the Dunker Church, he was shot in the foot and taken off the battlefield. He was critical of General George McClellan's cautious, piecemeal management of the situation that day. In January 1863 President Lincoln appointed him the new commander of the Army of the Potomac, replacing Ambrose Burnside.

Major General Joseph K. F. Mansfield Born in New Haven, Connecticut, Joseph Mansfield was a career soldier, graduating second in his West Point class in 1822. Although he had four decades of army service, he lacked combat experience when he arrived in Sharpsburg with his Twelfth Corps, of which he took command only two days before the battle. Hit in the stomach while leading his men through the East Woods, Mansfield died of his wounds two days later. He was buried in Middletown, Connecticut.

Major General George B. McClellan Born in Philadelphia, George McClellan graduated second in his class at West Point (1846), served in the Mexican-American War, and resigned from the army in 1857. After a successful civilian career as a railroad engineer and executive, he took command of an Ohio regiment in 1861, was put in charge of all the forces protecting Washington, D.C., and was elevated to commanding general. Although he formed a good battle strategy in advance of the Battle of Antietam, because of piecemeal deployment of troops, he failed to destroy Lee's army, although he successfully put a stop to Lee's Maryland campaign. President Lincoln's frustration with McClellan's inability to act, particularly after Antietam, when McClellan took his time in pursuing the Confederate army, resulted in his removal from command. Some years after the war, Ulysses S. Grant was asked to assess McClellan. "McClellan is to me one of the mysteries of the war," he stated.

Brigadier General George G. Meade Born in
Spain, George Meade attended West Point (1835)
and quit the military in 1836 after serving in the
Seminole War to work as a civil engineer. Find-
ing it difficult to support a large family as a civilian
engineer, he rejoined the army in 1842, where he
became a specialist in coastal engineering, building a handful of lighthouses on the east coast. He
and his division of the First Corps distinguished
themselves during the Battle of South Mountain,
and a few days later at Antietam, he replaced the
badly wounded General Hooker to command the
First Corps. Meade was wounded in the thigh at
Antietam. He recovered and went on to defeat
General Lee at Gettysburg, the feat for which he is
best known.

Brigadier General Edwin V. "Bull" Sumner Not
the brightest of leaders, Edwin Sumner had a reputation as being persistent in battle. His nickname
derived from his booming voice and a story that a
musket ball had once bounced off his head. Born
in Boston, he was the oldest field commander to
serve in the Civil War—he was sixty-five years old
at Antietam. He personally led one division of the
Second Corps at Antietam into the West Woods,
where they were ambushed, resulting in about
2,200 casualties. Sumner died of a heart attack the
next year.

Key Participants

Antietam National Battlefield: A Historical Tour

"The battle made quite a change in the look of the country. The fences and other familiar landmarks was [sic] gone, and you couldn't hardly tell one man's farm from another, only by the buildings, and some of them was burnt. You might be out late in the day and the dark would ketch you, and things was so torn and tattered that you didn't know nothin'. It was a strange country to you. I got lost three or four times when I thought I could go straight home. . . . Another queer thing was the silence after the battle. You couldn't hear a dog bark nowhere, you couldn't hear no birds whistle or no crows caw. There wa'n't no birds around till the next spring. We didn't even see a buzzard with all the stench."
—**From Johnson, Clifton,** ***Battleground Adventures.*** **Boston and New York: Houghton Mifflin Company, 1915.**

With its white clapboard and limestone houses and solid church buildings, Sharpsburg, Maryland, the site of the bloodiest single day in American history, feels like it has changed little since the day the famous battle took place in the late summer of 1862. Despite the tremendous tourist draw of the battlefield and the town, it feels as if time has stopped here. For many it did: An estimated 22,720 men were killed, wounded, captured, or missing after twelve hours of battle at Antietam in the fields surrounding Sharpsburg. In the days that followed, local people were left with the burden of burying the dead and tending to the wounded of both armies. For them life changed and would never be the same.

The town has remained so undeveloped that it is difficult to find a meal or a bed in or near Sharpsburg. So the best approach to visiting

Lutheran church in Sharpsburg after the battle.

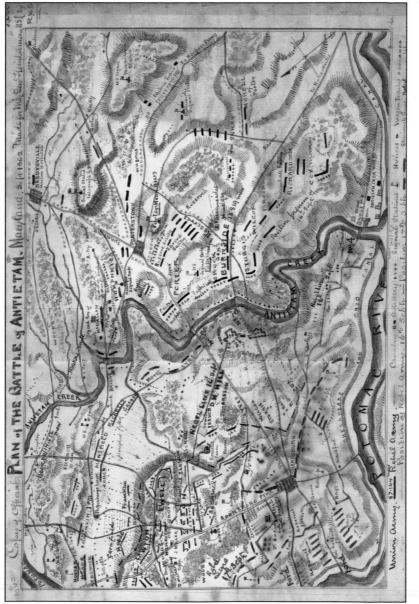

Plan of the Battle of Antietam showing the positions of Union and Confederate forces September 16 to September 17, 1862.

Sharpsburg, September 19, 1862.

Antietam National Battlefield is to plan to spend a full day here. If you bring a picnic lunch and arrive early, you will have plenty of time to participate in the excellent introductory programs that the National Park Service, which cares for and maintains the site, offers visitors, and you'll also be able to spend plenty of time touring the battlefield before the gates close after sunset.

Start your tour at the visitor center to see the exhibitions and the films offered there. The visitor center is located just north of Sharpsburg, just off of the Sharpsburg Pike (Route 65) on the western side of the battlefield. *Antietam Visit* is a twenty-six-minute film, shown in the visitor center every hour, that re-creates the Battle of Antietam and the visit of President Abraham Lincoln to General George B. McClellan in Sharpsburg after the battle in early October 1862. A second film, *Antietam,* narrated by James Earl Jones

Antietam

A line of cannons leads to the visitor center.

The Maryland State monument.

and filmed on the battlefield, is an excellent one-hour introduction for any visitor to the park. It's shown every day at noon. These films provide a great introduction to the Maryland Campaign, the battlefield, and the events that occurred there.

Additionally, Battlefield Orientation Talks are given by the friendly park staff every day, and during the summer additional talks, walks, and tours are added to the schedule. Check at the visitor-center reception desk for the day's schedule.

In the bookstore, located in the visitor center, you can purchase guidebooks, maps, and a self-guided 8½-mile tour of the battlefield with eleven well-marked tour stops that the park has set up. Playing the recorded battle tour in a car or on a personal audio player allows visitors to follow the events independently. Many visitors drive the route in their cars, but walking and biking are also great ways to tour the battlefield. Personalized and

As you tour the battlefield avenues, be sure to stop to read the markers and narrative tablets and have a close look at the ninety-six monuments that mark battle positions—they will help to bring the rich history of this battlefield alive. Cannons on the battlefield mark key artillery positions.

UNION MONUMENTS

1	IN 7th Infantry	49	CT 14th Infantry
2	PA 7th Reserve (36th Infantry)	50	MD 5th Infantry, Cos. A & I
4	PA 4th Reserve (33rd Infantry)	51	DE 1st Infantry
5	PA 3rd Reserve (32nd Infantry)	52	MD 5th Infantry
6	PA 8th Reserve (37th Infantry)	53	PA 130th Infantry
7	PA 12th Cavalry	54	IN 14th Infantry
10	PA 124th Infantry	55	OH 8th Infantry
11	NJ 13th Infantry	56	PA 132nd Infantry
12	IN State	58	DE 2nd Infantry
13	NJ State	59	NJ Hexamer's Battery
14	VT Company E & H 2nd U.S.S.S.	61	Irish Brigade: NY 63rd, 69th,
15	NY 84th (14th Brooklyn Infantry)		88th; MA 29th
16	NY 104th Infantry	64	IN 3rd Cavalry
17	PA 128th Infantry	67	U.S. Soldier ("Old Simon")
18	PA 137th Infantry	68	NY 20th Infantry
19	IN 27th Infantry	69	NY 4th Infantry
20	MD 1st Light Battery B	70	VT Company F, 1st U.S.S.S.
21	NJ 1st Brigade	71	PA 50th Infantry
22	BH 13th Infantry	72	PA 45th Infantry
23	MA State	73	PA 100th Infantry
26	PA 90th Infantry	74	OH 36th Infantry
27	DE 3rd Infantry	75	NY 9th Infantry (Hawkin's Zouaves)
28	IN 19th Infantry	77	CT 8th Infantry
29	NJ 1st Brigade	78	OH 28th Infantry
30	MA 15th Infantry	79	PA 51st Infantry
31	Philadelphia Brigade	80	PA Durrell's Battery D
35	NJ Hexamer's Battery	81	PA 48th Infantry
36	MD Battery A Light	82	OH 11th Infantry
37	NY 59th Infantry	83	MA 21st Infantry
38	NJ 13th Infantry	84	MA 35th Infantry
39	PA 125th Infantry	85	PA 51st Infantry
40	NY 34th Infantry	86	MD 2nd Infantry
41	MD Purnell Legion	87	NY 51st Infantry
42	MD State	88	CT 11th Infantry
43	OH 5th, 7th, 66th Infantry	91	OH 23rd Infantry
44	NY State	92	OH 30th Infantry
45	NY 20th Infantry	93	CT 16th Infantry
46	MD 3rd Infantry	94	OH 12th Infantry
48	Old Vermont Brigade	96	OH 1st Battery Light

CONFEDERATE MONUMENTS

24	TX State
25	GA State
33	MD, Baltimore Battery
62	Army of North VA, 6th VA Infantry
89	MD 1st, Dements's Battery

MORTUARY CANNONS

9	Major General Mansfield
34	Brigadier General Starke
57	Brigadier General Anderson
60	Major General Richardson
76	Major General Rodman
90	Brigadier General Branch

INDIVIDUAL MONUMENTS

3	Clara Barton
8	Major General Mansfield
32	Lt. Colonel J.L. Stetson (59th NY)
47	O.T. Reilly
63	Robert E. Lee
65	Colonel J.H. Childs, 4th PA Cavalry
66	Lee's Headquarters
95	William McKinley

Mondell Road

Mondell Road

66 34

Millers Sawmill Road

POTOMAC RIVER

34

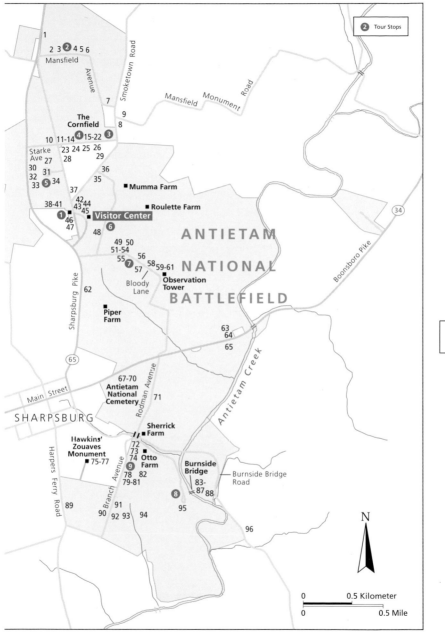

1

2 3 ② 4 5 6
Mansfield

Smoketown Road

Avenue

Mansfield Monument Road

7

The
Cornfield

9
8

10 11-14 ④ 15-22 ③

Starke 23 24 25 26
Ave 27 28 29
30 31
32 36
33 ⑤ 34 35
37

■ Mumma Farm

38-41 42 44
43 45 ■ Roulette Farm
① 46
47 ⑥

48

ANTIETAM

49 50
51-54
55 56
⑦ 58 59-61
57 ■ Observation
Tower
Bloody
62 Lane

NATIONAL

BATTLEFIELD

■ Piper
Farm

Sharpsburg Pike

Boonsboro Pike

34

② Tour Stops

63
64
65

Antietam Creek

65

67-70
Antietam
National
Cemetery

Rodman Avenue

71

Main Street

SHARPSBURG

Sherrick
■ Farm

Hawkins'
Zouaves
Monument
■ 75-77

72
73
74 ■ Otto
Farm
⑨ Burnside
78 82 Bridge
79-81 83-
⑧ 87 88

Burnside Bridge
Road

Harpers Ferry Road

Branch Avenue

89 91
90 92 93 94

95

96

N

0 0.5 Kilometer
0 0.5 Mile

25

A Guided Tour through History

A great way to help the National Park Service maintain the many monuments and memorials on the Antietam battlefield is to contact Adopt-a-Monument, Antietam National Battlefield, P.O. Box 158, Sharps-burg, MD 21782, (301) 432-2243.

specialty tours can also be arranged for a fee. For information about tours, please visit www .antietambattlefieldguides.com.

The visitor-center facilities and most of its exhibits are wheelchair accessible and open daily (except Thanksgiving, December 25, and January 1). The park closes twenty minutes after sunset. Fees for a three-day pass are $4 per person, $6 for families. An annual pass can be purchased for $20.

The battlefield, located to the north and east of the town, sprawls among farm fields and woods. On a bright, sunny day, this landscape is particularly beautiful. Considered the best preserved of all the American battle sites, as the landscape comes closest to looking the way it probably did at the start of the famous battle fought here, the National Park Service has worked hard to keep it pristine with ongoing programs of restoration. It is important to remember that

Antietam battlefield just after the fight.

A paved avenue at Antietam battlefield.

Antietam battlefield, where so many died or disappeared in battle, is hallowed ground. So visitors should note the regulations that the National Park Service has set up to help promote safety and preserve the battlefield:

- While touring the park, be alert to traffic and park only in the places designated for this purpose in the park.
- Bicyclists should use caution when descending hills.
- Please use trails to avoid stinging nettles, ticks, and snakes.
- Do not climb on cannons, monuments, fences, or trees.
- Relic hunting is prohibited.

Visitors can get more information by contacting Antietam National Battlefield, P.O. Box 158, Sharpsburg, MD 21782, (301) 432-5124, www.nps.gov/anti.

Sharpsburg: A Strong Battle Position

On September 15, 1862, near Sharpsburg, Maryland, when General Robert E. Lee was told at sunrise that the surrender of Harpers Ferry to Confederate troops was imminent, he made a decision that would change history. Worried that his military plans to press more deeply into the North had been compromised after the events at the Battle of South Mountain during the preceding days, he'd sent word to his commanders the previous night that they were to prepare to re-cross the Potomac and head back to Virginia. But upon receiving the unexpected good news that morning, Lee changed his mind, proclaiming, "We will make our stand on these hills."

After South Mountain, General Lee had plenty about which to worry. Colonel Clement Evans, who fought with the Thirty-fifth Georgia, wrote about the condition of the Confederate troops as the Battle of Antietam became imminent:

> *It is difficult to describe the condition of the troops at this time, so great and various was their wretchedness. They were sunburnt, gaunt, ragged, scarcely at all shod. . . . [They] had been scorched by the sultriest sun of the year, had been drenched with the rain and heavy dews peculiar to this latitude, had lost much night rest, had worn out their clothing and shoes, and received nothing but they could pick up on the battlefield. They had thrown away their knapsacks and blankets, in order to travel light; had fed on half-cooked dough, often raw bacon as well as raw beef; had devoured green corn and green apples, and contracted diarrhea and dysentery of the most malignant type. They now stood, an emaciated, limping, ragged mass, whom no stranger to their gallant exploits could have believed capable of anything the least worthy.*

—From Clement A. Evans, ed., *Confederate Military History.* **Atlanta: Confederate Publishing Company, 1899.**

Middle Bridge on Antietam Creek.

Sharpsburg citizens leaving before the battle.

Sharpsburg, sitting in a valley at the western base of the Sharpsburg Ridge, provided an excellent defensive position where Lee could wage war with the Federals with his army's flanks anchored on water both to the west, where the winding Potomac River flowed, and to the east, where there were plenty of places to ford the Antietam Creek. Artillery placed on the heights could be positioned ideally to defend the open fields broken up by patches of woodland below. To the west and north were outcroppings of rock and woodland that could be used as natural fortifications. The only drawback was that there was only one place close enough to escape back across the Potomac, if those circumstances should arise.

As Confederate troops began to enter Sharpsburg, the population was in great distress and citizens packed up everything they could and left. Mr. Waud, a reporter for *Harper's Weekly,* wrote this account for the October 11, 1862, edition of the paper, alluding to the tensions that would be directed at Confederate sympathizers after the fight:

Sharpsburg contains a population of about 2000, mostly Union people, the exceptions being very few. It suffered considerably in the recent battle, several buildings being burned, one of them being destroyed by the carelessness of the rebel soldiers who were cooking in it. All that was eatable they ate up; blankets they stole, and furniture they destroyed, even digging up things which the inhabitants had cached. Most of the citizens left the town with the women and children, hiding in the surrounding country till the rebel horde had left. A few secessionists, who remained and pointed out to the Southern rabble the houses of prominent Union men, it is to be hoped will be dealt with as they deserve. It would be a good idea to confiscate their goods for the benefit of the sufferers.

At noon, when another courier arrived with news that the Union garrison at Harpers Ferry had surrendered to General Stonewall Jackson, Lee sent a message to his scattered army to march to Sharpsburg as soon as possible. Lee would start this battle with less than 18,000 men, but General George B. McClellan, commander of the Army of the Potomac, believed Lee had at least twice, if not three times, that number.

Couriers were sent to Jackson and Hill to come to us as soon as possible. Our numbers in their absence are fearfully small, hardly 15,000 men, being those of Longstreet, D. H. Hill and Stuart's cavalry; and McClellan has 100,000; but they must be but hastily raised militia regiments, and don't count for much. Where do all these men come from?

—**Confederate Lieutenant William Miller Owen, in the vanguard of Confederate advance to Sharpsburg.**

The Confederate Line Forms

Lee's men entered Sharpsburg from Boonsboro that same morning of September 15, 1862, and began to form their lines on the Sharpsburg Ridge, extending about 3 miles north of the town just beyond Nicodemus Hill, the most commanding position over the open ground below, which would become the battlefield. Artillery was placed in significant spots along the ridge—there were about 200 Confederate guns on the day of the battle. Brigadier General John Hood and two brigades held the key position from the Dunker Church, where the fighting on the day of the battle would begin, northwest to Nicodemus Hill.

They were reinforced on September 16 by the arrival from Harpers Ferry of Jackson's troops, with Jackson taking command that day of the front, north of Sharpsburg. Cavalry commanded by J. E. B. Stuart protected the left flank of the Confederate line. D. H. Hill's five brigades were put in a position just south of the Dunker Church and extended their watch all the way to Sharpsburg, roughly following the path of the Hagerstown Pike. General James Longstreet's force, just north of Sharpsburg, reinforced the line another mile south to protect the road to Harpers Ferry. Brigadier General Nathan Evans took the center of the line near Sharpsburg with his brigade fixed on either side of the Boonsboro Pike. Major General D. R. Jones and his six brigades were responsible for the position southeast of Sharpsburg extending about

Currier and Ives print of the Battle of Sharpsburg, better known as Antietam.

a mile to Antietam Creek and the Lower or Rohrbach Bridge, which was renamed Burnside Bridge after the battle. John Walker's division took a position south of Sharpsburg when it arrived from Harpers Ferry on the sixteenth. Colonel Thomas Munford's cavalry was to guard all the Antietam Creek fords on the right of the Confederate line.

All of Lee's army, but A. P. Hill's division, was reunited by the sixteenth, so its number increased to a total of about 25,000 men. As one of Hill's officers summarized Lee's force after South Mountain, "None but heroes are left." By September 16, McClellan had gathered about 55,000 troops with another 14,000 just 6 miles away from Sharpsburg.

McClellan's Plan

General McClellan arrived at noon on September 15 and established headquarters on the east side of Antietam, but he sent out no cavalry to see where the enemy might be and no skirmishers to test its strength. Two bridges over the Antietam Creek near Union headquarters remained unprotected, as did the fords.

General McClellan among his admirers.

McClellan had now missed every opportunity to crush the Confederates since Special Order 191, Lee's battle plan for his Maryland Campaign, was discovered by the Yankees on September 13. Now the Confederate army that had been dispersed three days earlier was showing almost its full force on Sharpsburg Ridge, a position McClellan knew Lee intended to hold. However, McClellan did not know and made no attempt to either find out Lee's true numbers, nor did he seek out precisely where the Confederate forces were gathering and positioning themselves.

Sergeant John M. Bloss, a Union soldier from Indiana, was one of the men that found Lee's Special Order 191. This is his account of what happened:

On September 13, Company F, 27th Indiana, was placed on the skirmish line in front of our brigade. We moved forward rapidly and soon reached the suburbs of Frederick. It was a warm morning and we threw ourselves upon the grass to rest. While lying there I noticed a large envelope. It was not sealed, and when I picked it up two cigars and a paper fell out. . . . The cigars were divided and, while the needed match was being secured, I began to read the enclosed document. As I read, each line became more interesting. It was Lee's order to his army, giving his plans for the next four days from that time and, if true, was exceedingly important. . . . The order made known not only Lee's position, but his intent. . . .

It showed that Lee proposed to divide his army on the 10th and that at this time, the 13th, it was really separated into five divisions and that three divisions were far away. . . .
—**First Sergeant John M. Bloss, Twenty-seventh Indiana Volunteer Infantry.**

McClellan spent September 16 planning his attack. His most aggressive commander, Major General Joseph "Fighting Joe" Hooker, leading the First Corps across the Antietam northeast of Sharpsburg, was to occupy a position along the Hagerstown Pike opposite the Confederate left. Major General Joseph Mansfield's Twelfth Corps, with Brigadier General Edwin V. Sumner's Second Corps, were to hold the Confederate line from Hooker's left, along the Smoketown Road and as far as Pry's Mill Ford on the Antietam. Major General Fitz-John Porter's Fifth Corps was to protect the center of the line along the Boonsboro Pike.

Once the Confederate left was engaged and if McClellan's plan succeeded, the rebel retreat was to be cut off by Ambrose Burnside's Ninth Corps, which was to fight across the Antietam at the Lower Bridge on the Confederate right, blocking off Lee's escape route to the Potomac. McClellan intended to hold two divisions in reserve, Fitz-John Porter's Fifth Corps and William B. Franklin's Sixth Corps, to exploit any Confederate breakthrough or

Lower Bridge, later called Burnside Bridge.

to meet any counterattack. He also planned to keep his large cavalry division in reserve. Four batteries of twenty-pound Parrott rifles, under Brigadier General Henry Jackson Hunt's command, were positioned just south of the Boonsboro Pike with other guns placed in key positions.

And if McClellan had succeeded in breaching the southern end of Lee's line, he intended to smash his way toward Sharpsburg and use all his army's force, driving it up the Boonsboro Road to destroy the Confederate center. If executed in a coordinated manner, this was a very good and logical plan, as the sheer power of Union numbers had the potential to stretch Lee's much smaller army gathered at Sharpsburg to the breaking point.

The Day before the Battle

McClellan ordered General Joseph Hooker's First Corps to cross Antietam Creek on September 16, 1862, and prepare to attack the Confederate army the next morning. Hooker's 12,000 men, just back from the tough fighting at Turner's Gap, moved out from their camp near Keedysville at 2:00 p.m. and crossed at the Upper Bridge. Passing through fields and using the cover of

Hooker's First Corps fords Antietam Creek.

the North Woods, First Corps moved north and west towards the Hagerstown Pike in the late afternoon, establishing their line on either side of the turnpike. With news that Union troops had crossed the Antietam, General Hood moved his line east of the turnpike through a cornfield and into the East Woods. Reserves were placed to Hood's left, extending the rebel line west across Hagerstown Pike.

Major General George Meade charged Hood's troops in the fading light of the day in the fields near the East Woods, but both sides were forced to take cover because of artillery fire. When darkness made it difficult to find a target, the fighting and shooting soon just died out. Hooker complained out loud, "If they had let us start earlier, we might have finished tonight."

That night Hooker settled down with his men on the farm of Joseph Poffenberger near the North Woods. "We are through for to-night, gentlemen," Hooker told George Washburn Smalley and his colleague Albert D. Richardson, reporters for the *New York Tribune,* "but to-morrow we fight the battle that will decide the fate of the Republic." Hooker notified McClellan that he would open the battle at dawn. A light rain fell through the night as the armies, now so close they could hear each other's footsteps, did what they could to get some sleep and prepare for what fate would bring the next day.

General Hooker's headquarters at Poffenberger Farm.

The New Jersey State Monument at sunset.

Frederick L. Hitchcock wrote the history of the 132nd Pennsylvania Volunteers, recording what may have gone on the night before on both sides as infantry bedded down for the night before the Battle of Antietam:

> Letters were written home—many of them "last words"—and quiet talks were had, and promises made between comrades. Promises providing against the dread possibilities of the morrow. . . . I can never forget the quiet words of Colonel Oakford, as he inquired very particularly if my roster of the officers and men of the regiment was complete, for, said he, with a smile, "We shall not all be here to-morrow night.
>
> —From Hitchcock, Frederick L., *War from the Inside: The Story of the 132nd Regiment Pennsylvania Volunteer Infantry in the War for the Suppression of the Rebellion.* Philadelphia: J. B. Lippincott, 1904.

Colonel Richard A. Oakford was killed the next day; Hitchcock survived to write his history.

Tour Stop 1

Dunker Church

It was gray, cool, and foggy at daybreak, which came at 5:43 a.m. on Wednesday, September 17, 1862. What the early morning mist concealed was most of the Confederate army that had reinforced and strengthened its line in the heights and on the ridge to the west. At 5:00 a.m. General Joe Hooker rode out to inspect the ground in front of his Union line. To the east of the Hagerstown Pike that lay in front of his First Corps, he saw the lines of Confederate guns on the high flat ground, where you can see the cannons on the rise near the visitor center. And just across the turnpike, Hooker fixed on the Dunker Church, the simple white building in front of you, named for a small religious sect

The battle near Dunker Church.

Civil War cannons on the high ground in front of Dunker Church.

The Union's artillery was a great obstacle for the Confederates. Often running low on ammunition throughout the long day, Rebel artillerymen, unlike their Yankee counterparts, often had to improvise when their shells ran out:
"Broken railroad iron and blacksmiths' tools, hammers, chisels &c., were fired from rebel cannon. Some of these missiles made a peculiar noise, resembling 'which away, which away,' by which the national troops came to distinguish them from the regular shot and shell, and as they heard them approaching, would cry, 'Turkey! Turkey coming!' and fall flat to avoid them. An artillerist, a German, when he saw the tools falling around him, exclaimed, 'My Got! we shall have the blacksmith's shop to come next!'"
—From Moore, Frank, *Anecdotes, Poetry, and Incidents of the War.* New York: The Arundel Print, 1882.

of pacifists—the German Baptist Brethren—who "dunked" believers to baptize them. If Hooker could take the church and the elevated plateau across the turnpike, he thought he would have a good chance at destroying the Army of Northern Virginia in fairly short order.

General McClellan had set up headquarters in tents, east of Antietam Creek on the property of Philip and Elizabeth Pry (today it's the Pry House Field Hospital Museum), about 2 miles from the farm where Hooker was positioned at the outset of the battle. Moving comfortable armchairs from the big house onto the lawn, McClellan and his staff prepared to observe the battle through telescopes from that position, which is where they watched the battle for most of the day.

At about 6:00 a.m. rebel cannons blasted from Nicodemus Hill at the top of the Confederate line and muskets opened fire from a position in front of the Dunker Church. An enormous barrage of Federal big guns, positioned in the hills above the Antietam and aimed at the Confederate left, responded. The Battle of Antietam had begun.

Tour Stop 2

North Woods

Hooker's 8,600 infantrymen of the First Corps advanced south with violence through the North Woods, near where you stand, and quickly were spread over the area stretching from the East Woods to the West Woods, both of which you can see from this spot to the east and west, respectively. While the Confederate guns on Nicodemus Hill were blasting away at them, Brigadier General Abner Doubleday's men charged down the Hagerstown Pike and Brigadier General James Ricketts's rushed toward the Dunker Church via the Smoketown Road. On the Confederate side there were 7,700 troops ready for the assault. Three of D. H. Hill's brigades jumped into action from the Sunken Road to support Stonewall Jackson's men, who formed an east-to-west line from the church, while Hood's brigades waited in the West Woods for Hooker's attack.

Artillery Hell by Captain James Hope illustrates the intensity of the Confederate artillery in front of Dunker Church and Nicodemus Hill (center) in the early stages of the battle.

Tour Stop 3

East Woods

The fighting that had begun in the East Woods the night before picked up again as soon as the first light of dawn appeared. Three of Meade's regiments moved out of the woods to the Smoketown Road, attacking Confederate troops, led by Colonel James Walker, in a freshly plowed field on the Mumma Farm to the south. The Thirteenth Pennsylvania, or the Bucktails as they were better known, were excellent mountain-bred marksmen and were all fired up that morning because their commander, Colonel Hugh W. McNeil, had been killed by the rebels in the East Woods the night before.

Smoketown Road and East Woods in the distance.

Concealing themselves behind trees and wooden fences, the Bucktails let loose a deadly stream of fire into Walker's troops, who could find little shelter in the Mumma field from the rifle fire or relief from the noise and distraction of the bombardment of the Union guns on the opposite side of the Antietam Creek. Ordered to pull back when the Bucktails' ammunition began to run low, another order went out in the confusion of smoke and noise, sending the Union troops out of the fight in which they had, until that chaotic moment, the advantage. As Walker's men pursued the Yankees into the East Woods, General James Ricketts's men reached Miller's Cornfield just yards to the north.

There were more men killed, wounded, or missing in one day of battle at Antietam than the total casualties in the War of 1812, the Mexican-American War, and the Spanish-American War combined.

Tour Stop 4

The Cornfield

When General Ricketts's lead brigade, commanded by Colonel Abram Duryea, got to the north edge of the twenty-acre Miller's Cornfield, which you see in front of you, they set up a battery to the east of Miller's orchard to support their hastily formed battle line on the cornfield's edge. Firing rounds of canister into the cornfield before they advanced, Duryea's 1,100 troops began cautiously to make their way into the field, where the corn stood as tall as a man.

Concealed in the pasture south of Miller's Cornfield were Brigadier General A. R. Lawton's Confederates, all lying down, some behind piles of fence rails. As the Yankees came out of the corn, the rebels stood up and hit them with everything

The cornfield.

they had. Union men, stumbling forward over their dead and wounded piling up, formed a line no more than 250 yards away from the Confederates, and each side began shooting away at the other. In the smoke, noise, and destruction, both armies began to lie down, and from that position, with no cover, continued to fire away at each other at close range.

With rebel fire now aimed at the Confederates from a rock ledge on one of their flanks and ammunition running low, Duryea ordered withdrawal back into the cornfield. In about thirty minutes of fighting, one-third of his 1,100 men had been shot. Rebel troops had also taken heavy casualties. Short on ammunition, those Confederates that survived pulled what they could find off dead soldiers and continued to fight.

While Duryea's men fought to the east, Doubleday's men on the Hagerstown Pike reached the western edge of Miller's Cornfield. Rebel soldiers hidden in the corn rose up and gunned down the Yankees who were advancing. Major Rufus Dawes of the Sixth Wisconsin was among Doubleday's men, and he reported, "Men, I cannot say fell; they were knocked out of the ranks by the dozens. But we jumped over the fence, and pushed on, loading, firing, and shouting as we advanced." General Joseph Hooker, having seen this surprise slaughter, also saw sunlight reflecting off the bayonets of the rebels concealed still deeper in the cornfield and directed any batteries he could to a spot to the left side of the field. From there the Union troops were ordered to blast the cornfield with canisters and shells. Hooker later wrote: "In the time that I am writing, every stalk of corn in the northern and greater part of the field was cut

"The field and its ghastly harvest which the reaper had gathered in those fatal hours remained finally with us. Four times it had been lost and won. The dead are strewn so thickly that as you ride over it you cannot guide your horse's steps too carefully. Pale and bloody faces are everywhere upturned. They are sad and terrible, but there is nothing which makes one's heart beat so quickly as the imploring look of sorely wounded men who beckon wearily for help which you cannot stay to give."
—**George Washburn Smalley's eyewitness account of the aftermath of the fighting in Miller's Cornfield as reported in the *New York Tribune*, September 19, 1862.**

Confederate dead on the Hagerstown Pike.

as closely as could have been done with a knife, and the slain lay in rows precisely as they had stood in their ranks a few moments before. It was never my fortune to witness a more bloody, dismal battlefield."

For three hours the battle raged violently that morning, shifting back and forth from the cornfield to the pasture to the south or the East Woods and back, neither side gaining anything, both sides just standing up to the bloody slaughter of the fighting. As Union batteries of guns positioned in front of the East Woods and in the cornfield dueled with the Confederate guns in front of Dunker Church, clouds of white smoke hung in the rising fog above the cornfield and troops of both sides just kept feeding into the awful fighting. Historian Stephen W. Sears writes that "in an hour and a half of fighting Hooker's command and Jackson's had been reduced to mutual shambles." Nor had Hooker received any support for his three divisions during that time period—Jackson and Lee just fed in more men, three divisions in the first part of the morning, as the fight dictated. Hood's Confederates faired the worst: Hood reported to Lee that "my division has been almost wiped out."

Survivors were stunned and utterly exhausted from the frenzy of the unusually close combat. Many who ran for their lives were shot down in their tracks and those who managed to get to the picket and rail fences that bounded the roads were stopped there, where the bodies piled up and hung on the fences. Battle-tested veterans on both sides remembered this as the worst fighting they'd ever lived through. The carnage was devastating.

A newspaper illustration showing the dead that fell near the picket fences near the cornfield.

AT THE FENCE.

Tour Stop 5

West Woods

While all this was taking place in the cornfield, General Ricketts's men had made their way to the southern end of the East Woods, where Captain Dunbar Ransom's artillerymen broke out from their wooded cover, blasting the surprised Confederates gathered in the vicinity of the Mumma Farm. Ricketts's and Doubleday's troops, now fairly deep into the Confederate line after more than an hour of strenuous battle on a field that stretched from the Mumma Farm through Miller's Cornfield and into the West Woods, were reinforced finally when General George Meade's men rushed into the fight. Then, just at that moment, Jackson counterattacked, beating the Union troops back to

The dead near Miller's Farm.

the cornfield, where the attackers were halted by heavy Union fire coming from the East Woods.

As General Joseph Hooker's men took shelter in the woods and while the Union battery in front blasted away, the heavy columns of Union Major General Joseph Mansfield's Twelfth Corps could be seen approaching from the north. Seeing the tough fight in and around the East Woods, Mansfield moved to the head to command his troops to attack and was instantly wounded, taking a bullet in the chest. He died two days later.

General Joseph Mansfield, a field commander for only a few days before Antietam, was one of six generals (three Union, three Confederate) killed or mortally wounded during the battle. The National Park Service has marked the places where they each fell with a mortuary cannon, a cannon barrel muzzle pointing down and set in a block of stone.

Without missing a single beat, Brigadier General Alpheus Williams stepped up and took command, pushing his force over the field that Hooker's men had held, while Brigadier General Samuel Crawford's men made their way down the Hagerstown Pike toward the West Woods. All were stopped or scattered by gunfire coming from the rocks and woods to the west and by J. E. B. Stuart's artillery on Nicodemus Hill to their rear. Jackson's worn-out Confederates were pushed back through the cornfield and then to the Dunker Church, where a big gap opened up in Lee's line.

Two Union Twelfth Corps brigades led by Brigadier General George S. Greene fought their way onto the raised plateau, about 200 yards from the Dunker Church. General Hooker ordered two of his First Corps batteries to move in support of a further advance by Greene's men. At about 9:00 a.m. Hooker, mounted on his white horse, rode through a pasture near the cornfield, seeing the opportunity now within reach that he had contemplated all morning of finally taking the ground he had fought hard for since sunrise.

However, before he could occupy the position, Hooker was shot in the foot by a Confederate sharpshooter. While he attempted to remain on the battlefield, he started feeling weak and faint from blood loss and was taken to the rear. General George Meade stepped in and took over Hooker's command. Hooker testified after the battle that when he left the field, he thought his men had enough numbers to finally break the Confederate line on the left. "I supposed that we had everything in our own hands."

For most of the anxious morning, General Robert E. Lee directed his men from a grove of trees, the Oak Grove, west of Sharpsburg and the battlefield, where he had set up headquarters and from where he could see part of the action. At sunrise he ordered the divisions commanded by Major General Lafayette McLaws and Colonel George T. Anderson, who had rapidly marched up from Harpers Ferry starting out at midnight, to rest before being sent into the battle. At 7:15 a.m. he had ordered, at Stonewall Jackson's request, James Longstreet's Georgia brigade, led by George T. Anderson, to move into the field to support Jackson as the fighting in the cornfield intensified. He also observed from his position that the Union troops located opposite the Lower Bridge were inactive.

After the hours of intense killing in Miller's Cornfield appeared to subside, Lee left his headquarters, riding out to position a line of guns on Hauser's Ridge, high above the position of the Dunker Church and to the west, to assess the situation. Halfway from Sharpsburg he encountered Colonel Stephen Lee, who had been sent by Hood to find Lee and request immediate reinforcement. "Don't be excited about it, Colonel. Go tell General Hood to hold his ground. Reinforcements are now

In the first four hours of the Battle of Antietam, total casualties were estimated at about 12,000 men. Five Union and four Confederate divisions were hit so hard in the first surge of the battle—the most intense fighting of the day—that they saw no more fighting on September 17, 1862.

"As one of the regiments was for the second time going into the conflict, a soldier staggered. It was from no wound, but in the group of dying and dead, through which they were passing, he saw his father, of another regiment, lying dead. There, too, was a wounded man who knew them both, who pointed to the father's corpse, and then upwards, saying only, 'It is all right with him.' Onward went the son, by his father's corpse, to do his duty in the line, which, with bayonets fixed, advanced upon the enemy."

—**From Moore, Frank,** *Anecdotes, Poetry, and Incidents of the War.* **New York: The Arundel Print, 1882.**

rapidly approaching between Sharpsburg and the ford. Tell him that I am coming to his support," Lee said, and as he rode off he pointed to the head of McLaws's column that he had ordered to march as he was leaving headquarters, along with Walker's two additional brigades that had been positioned all morning near the Lower Bridge. These reinforcements moved north with speed into the West Woods, where 10,000 Confederates, joining General Jubal Early's brigade already there and under Stonewall Jackson's command, took cover behind the outcrops of rocks and clumps of trees to hide themselves, off to the west from where you stand.

Major General Edwin Sumner's Second Corps appeared out of the East Woods, just after Hooker was wounded. General John Sedgwick's division was in the lead and, with Sumner in command, the decision was made to attack the worn-out Confederates immediately, not realizing that Brigadier General William French's division was not following close behind. Marching through part of the cornfield in a tight column and crossing the Hagerstown Pike, the Second Corps moved into the western side of the West Woods and marched right into an ambush.

From their left flank, the Yankees were hit suddenly with a wall of gunfire at point-blank range coming from two of Jackson's divisions—about 10,000 soldiers—that encircled them in the woods that you see here. The attack created mass confusion among the Union soldiers, and about 2,500, or half of Sedgwick's men, died or were wounded in only twenty minutes.

Surviving Union men, the regiments that had been positioned mainly on the Federal right, fled to the northeast, while Jackson's troops fired after them. Sedgwick's artillery in the cornfield and more batteries in the East Woods offered these stunned survivors cover. Jackson counterattacked, charging across the fields and hitting the Federal batteries positioned in front of the East Woods. But the heavy Union fire stopped Jackson and the rebel troops ran back for cover in the West Woods.

Greene, whose men were now running low on ammunition, continued to hold the ground near the Dunker Church to the south, while Sedgwick's men struggled in the West Woods. Supplies and support from cannons handled by a Rhode Island battery under Captain John A. Tompkins arrived just in time, at virtually the same moment as South Carolina rebels counterattacked, taking heavy losses. Soon there was another attempt by the Confederates, attacking out of the West Woods, to

After Sumner's charge.

Confederate dead in a rifle ditch.

dislodge Greene. Concealed behind the rise of the plateau, Greene's men waited until the rebel troops were within 70 yards and tore up the charge, sending survivors running back to the woods for cover. The Yankees pursued and moved into a position 200 yards beyond the Dunker Church, also securing the area behind them that they had so tenaciously held. Greene then sent out an urgent call for reinforcements.

Tour Stop 6

Union Advance

General Edwin Sumner's two other divisions of the Union Second Corps, led by General William French, had crossed the Antietam due east of the Dunker Church at the Pry's Mill Ford, following about twenty minutes behind Sedgwick's troops. When French reached the East Woods, Sumner was nowhere in sight, and French, without orders and with no support, made the decision to move to the southwest, toward the Roulette Farmhouse near the Confederate center, probably to support the Union Twelfth Corps that could be seen in the distance, to your left, near the Dunker Church. General Lee watched with D. H. Hill behind the Confederate center, as French's men moved through the battlefield. What French did not know as he moved forward was that he, with his 5,700 troops with banners flying (and "with all the precision of a parade day," Hill later wrote), was opening up a new sector of the Antietam battlefront.

General William French.

French's men marched south through the fields of the Mumma Farm and through the pastures and apple orchard of the Roulette farmstead, where you see the farmhouse that still stands to your northeast. They chased off rebel skirmishers from the farm buildings, but the route ahead was wide open and provided no cover. Just past the Roulette property, the ground, as you can see, rises to a low ridge that runs along the front of the Sunken Road, a worn-down farm road about half a mile long and about 500 yards away from the Dunker

53

A Guided Tour through History

Sunken Road today.

Church. The old road is a natural trench formed
by erosion and the weight of heavy wagons laden
with grain hauled for generations to a gristmill
on Antietam Creek. A naturally formed defensive
position, the Bloody Lane, as the first 1,000 yards
of the Sunken Road came to be called, helped
Confederate troops positioned there to beat back
waves of Union attacks over the next four hours of
intense, brigade-sized charges.

In the trench were what remained of D. H. Hill's
five brigades, or about 2,500 soldiers, who had
been dispersed, fighting all over the battlefield
that morning. But Hill had collected his men at
the Sunken Road now and there they lay in wait
at about 10:30 a.m. for the advance of French's
troops up the ridge, as the wind picked up and
began to blow away the morning's haze.

Tour Stop 7

Sunken Road

Sumner's divisions attacked the Sunken Road frontally with an extraordinary barrage of fire, took heavy casualties, and fell back. French's troops in the rear moved up, quickly enveloping the stunned survivors, and rushed forward to attack. Major

Sunken Road, 1896.

General Israel Richardson's division, part of Sumner's corps led by the Irish Brigade of New York, was marching to support Greene at the Dunker Church. Approaching on French's left, the attention of the New Yorkers turned suddenly to hitting Hill's right flank.

Lee, seeing the action and knowing the consequences if the Sunken Road was lost, quickly ordered up Major General R. H. Anderson's division, knowing it would need time to reach the fight. Brigadier General Robert Rodes provided it by launching a crushing attack on French's men to prevent them from supporting Richardson, who prepared to attack the Confederates in the Sunken Road. Despite French's setback, Richardson, known to be tough as nails, rushed to the Sunken Road and charged the Confederates on the crest of the ridge with fury. As soon as Anderson arrived behind Hill's men, and before he could put his 3,400 men into action, he dropped, wounded in the ankle. The Confederate surge, then, began to lose its force.

"One of the sights not to be forgotten, was that of a Confederate trying to escape to the rear across a rail fence on the west side of the sunken road; he had his right foot across the rail, the left in a partial kneeling position, with one hand holding a piece of apple in his mouth, shot dead transfixed and erect with seven bullet holes in his back."

—From *War Papers Read Before the Michigan Commandery of the Military Order of the United States,* by Charles C. Coffin, read January 7, 1897.

A Guided Tour through History

The dead in Bloody Lane.

"On looking about me I found that we were in an old sunken road and that the bed of it lay from one to three feet below the surface of the crest along which it ran. In this road there lay so many dead rebels that there formed a line which one might have walked on as far as I could see, many of whom had been killed by the most horrible wounds of shot and shell and they lay just as they had been killed apparently amid the blood which was soaking the earth. It was on this ghastly flooring that we kneeled for the last struggle."
—**Lt. Thomas Leonard Livermore, serving with the Fifth New Hampshire Infantry.**

At the top of the Sunken Road, some confusion in orders by General Robert Rodes caused the soldiers in the trench to begin withdrawing to the rear. An attack by the Twenty-ninth Massachusetts set off another confused chain reaction of retreat in the Confederate lines in another section of the trench. While some rebel troops were being extricated to relieve crowding, word spread that a retreat had been ordered and men began to leave the trench around noon. In one minute a stampede was on and the Confederate line began to fall apart. Many fleeing men were gunned down, while others withdrew to the rear, opening up a huge hole in the Confederate front. Watching this confusion, Colonel Francis C. Barlow swiftly positioned his two regiments, the Sixty-first and Sixty-fourth New York, on either side of the road at the rear of the line and ordered them to sweep the length of the Sunken Road with gunfire.

General McClellan, watching from his headquarters at the Pry house, had a good view of the battle fought in the Bloody Lane (Sunken Road). Reporting for the *Boston Journal,* Charles Coffin filed this report:

Up the slope moves the line to the top of a knoll. Ah! what a crash! A white cloud, gleams of lightning, a yell, a hurrah, and then up in the corn-field a great commotion, men firing into each other's faces, the Confederate line breaking, the ground strewn with prostrate forms. General McClellan was exultant. "It is the most beautiful field I ever saw, and the grandest battle!"

Those Confederate soldiers that survived had a tough time removing themselves from the bodies that had dropped around them. The slaughtered

dead and wounded rebels were piled up in the trench, which had now earned a new label: the Bloody Lane.

The Bloody Lane.

Union casualties were heavy, too, with dead and wounded carpeting the approaches to either side of the trench. Photographs taken after the battle confirm eyewitness reports that the bodies were so thick, particularly in the Bloody Lane, that a man could walk as far as one could see upon the corpses without ever touching the ground. Both Barlow and Richardson—Richardson died of his wounds—were badly wounded along with dozens more officers from both sides. At 1:00 p.m., after about two hours of exhausting and violent fighting, the battlefield suddenly went quiet again.

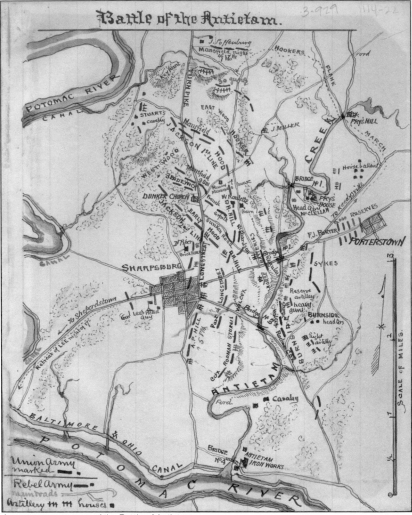

A contemporary map of the Battle of Antietam.

Those Confederates who could, fled, retreating south in the direction of Sharpsburg; D. H. Hill rushed to prevent a Yankee breakthrough to the town. Longstreet also tried to bring some order to the chaos and formed a new line on the Hagerstown Pike. But the center of Lee's line was wide open with his army divided into two parts. If hit quickly and hard, the Confederate army could easily have been annihilated at that moment. With Franklin's Sixth Corps primed and ready for attack, McClellan held back, deciding to take the defensive.

Lee, on the other hand, quickly made a plan to launch an attack against the Union flank positioned in the North Woods and just beyond in the East Woods. The desired result was to relieve the pressure on D. H. Hill's troops, who might then push the Union troops to the Antietam and score a demoralizing defeat. It never occurred to Lee that McClellan had stopped his attack after the fight at the Bloody Lane. So in the early afternoon, Stonewall Jackson and J. E. B. Stuart made their plans to attack the Union lines in the north. But when they reached the battlefield, they determined that the Union artillery on the ridge, east of the Middle Bridge, was so strong that their plan would quickly be stopped. So Lee's mind now focused south.

Antietam was the first American battlefield in history to be photographed before the battle's dead were buried. Alexander Gardner and his assistant, James Gibson, who worked for the famous Civil War photographer Matthew Brady, took seventy photos at Antietam two days after the battle. When they were reproduced in newspapers, using woodcuts made from the photo images, with accounts of the battle, the images transformed American's perception of war by showing the grim reality of the battlefield. In early October Gardner returned to Antietam and took the famous photos of President Lincoln's meeting with General McClellan. When Gardner's original battle images were displayed in Brady's New York gallery, the New York Times reported, "If he has not brought bodies and laid them in our dooryards and along streets, he has done something very like it."

Tour Stop 8

Lower Bridge (Burnside Bridge)

General Ambrose E. Burnside's Ninth Corps had moved south in the direction of the Lower Bridge, which you see below, on the morning of September 17. McClellan had ordered Burnside to get his men ready for an attack early that day across the Antietam Creek, but as the day passed, no orders came. And Lee, seeing no activity in this part of the field earlier that day, was able to shift a division and a brigade from this position on his right to his left with no resistance—the same troops that had moved up to ambush Sedgwick's men in the West Woods.

Burnside Bridge.

The charge across Burnside Bridge.

The bridge itself was defended by several hundred of Brigadier General Robert Toombs's Georgia men, who were positioned in rifle pits dug into an abandoned quarry on the heavily wooded west side of the creek overlooking the bridge. Although Burnside had about 13,000 troops here, as opposed to Lee's 4,000, the Confederates possessed a very strong position on the high ground above Antietam Creek, from which they poured down fire on anything that approached the bridge.

Just after 9:00 a.m. McClellan's men began their assault on the bridge, but Georgia guns thwarted each attempt. At 10:00 a.m. Burnside still had not gotten a single man across the creek. By noon, after repeated attempts to get across (and when the battle at the Sunken Road was at its most fierce), Union troops still had neither taken the bridge nor found a way across the creek, only 30 yards wide and relatively shallow.

Finally, a Union division commanded by Brigadier General Isaac Rodman, his men working their way cautiously downstream, discovered a crossing at Snavely's Ford, about a mile south of the bridge. Rodman crossed the creek and began an attack on the right flank of the Confederates defending the bridge. Colonel George Crook also sent out scouts, and at about the same time as Rodman, his brigade crossed the Antietam a little north of the bridge.

At 1:00 p.m. the Fifty-first New York and the Fifty-first Pennsylvania regiments charged and finally fought their way across the bridge itself, supported by artillery. As masses of Union troops pushed their way across the bridge, Crook and Rodman hit the Confederate flanks, breaking the soldiers from Georgia. After four hours, Burnside succeeded at last in reaching the west side of the creek.

But once across, the Yankees in the lead found that they were short on ammunition and had to go back for more, slowing progress considerably and underlining the management problems that appeared to cause the morning's lack of progress.

Tour Stop 9

The Final Attack

Not until 3:00 p.m. did Ambrose Burnside get his whole command moving into the hills and fields to the south of Sharpsburg. The Ninth New York Zouaves pushed farthest forward and took the greatest bashing, fighting their way through extremely heavy resistance, at times hand-to-hand, with many dropping in their tracks as they advanced. The monument you see in the distant field marks the Zouaves' position and is a memorial to these brave men, 63 percent of whom died in the advance. The Confederates put up stout resistance, but finally gave way before overwhelming the Union numbers. They were forced back into the town of Sharpsburg, to which every other rebel infantry unit that fought that day had withdrawn.

Lee tried to stop the Union drive toward Sharpsburg by moving all his artillery in a southerly

Twenty medals of honor were awarded to Antietam veterans. The youngest, fifteen-year-old bugler John Cook from Cincinnati, stepped up and helped Battery B, Fourth U.S. Artillery, load canisters into a twelve-pound Napoleon gun to provide support for the Union Iron Brigade (also known as the Black Hats) fighting near the Miller Farm under the command of General "Fighting Joe" Hooker the morning of the battle.

The Ninth New York Zouaves on the right flank of the Confederates. The town of Sharpsburg can be seen in the distance.

direction. Just as Burnside threatened to capture the Harpers Ferry Road, the Confederate escape route across the Potomac, just south of Sharpsburg and only half a mile away, Lee noticed a cloud of dust on the horizon. Then, marching men began to appear to the south. It was A. P. Hill's Light Division, flying the Virginia and Confederate flags, arriving after a seven-hour forced march from Harpers Ferry.

Hill's five brigades smashed into the inexperienced Sixteenth Connecticut, positioned on the Union flank; these green troops broke and ran, and other Union regiments followed them as they fled to the banks of the Antietam to get away from this unexpected attack and the Confederate artillery showering down. Further confusion was created

Antietam

This is the account of a slave woman, the cook at Delaney's Tavern, in the center of Sharpsburg, who spent the whole day of the battle in the cellar of the tavern:

I was back workin' in the kitchen, but the soldiers told me I'd better get out, and then all of us in the house went into the cellar. We carried boards down there and spread carpets on 'em and took chairs down to set on. There were seven or eight of us, white and black, and we was all so scared we did n't know what we was doin' half the time. They kept us in the cellar all day while they was fightin' backwards and forwards. My gooness [sic] alive! There was cannon and everything shootin'. . . . The cannon sounded just like thunder, and the small-arms the same as pop-guns. Sometimes we'd run up and look out of a window to see what was happening, but we didn't do that often—not the way them guns was firin'. . . . After they'd fit all day and it got to be night they ceased fightin' and was n't doin' much shootin', and then we come up. . . . At last the Rebels retreated and we heard 'em hollerin'. I spoke to one of 'em who was passin', and said, "Did you have a hard fight to-day?" "Yes, Aunty," he said, "the Yankees give us the devil, and they'll give us hell next."

—From Johnson, Clifton, *Battleground Adventures.* Boston and New York: Houghton Mifflin Company, 1915.

by the fact that some of Hill's troops wore new blue Union uniforms that they had acquired at Harpers Ferry; they also carried a captured American flag, so many Union troops were tricked into holding their fire as Hill's men approached.

The Union right flank, however, still held and was threatening a weak Confederate position to the east of Sharpsburg. With the support Burnside was promised by McClellan, who watched what was happening as Fitz-John Porter's Fifth Corps and the cavalry stood by, Lee's line could have been broken, despite the miracle of A. P. Hill's eleventh-hour intervention. But McClellan did not act.

An hour and a half after Hill's unexpected arrival, all action stopped as the sun set on the horrific battlefield, thick with the dead and the dying. In the dark of night the sounds of the dying and wounded were heartbreaking and haunting, and the smell of vomit, blood, decaying flesh, and excrement that rose off the battlefield, repulsive. But as the sun rose on the morning of September 18, it was the unforgettable image of miles of battlefield, carpeted with bodies and body parts, wounded who had not been attended to, dead animals, and knapsacks, guns, spent shells, and bloody clothing, that shocked witnesses. How could all of this sacrifice for a battle that ended with no victor be justified?

The Next Day

Despite the devastation and terrible things witnessed by those who survived the actions of the previous day, there remained 30,000 Confederate

The *New York Tribune* report about George Washburn Smalley's eyewitness account of the Battle of Antietam was the first to reach the outside world in print form. Published only thirty-six hours after the battle on September 19, it is considered a masterpiece of battle reporting, in no small part due to its accuracy. Smalley, posing as a Union aide-de-camp, tagged along with General Joseph Hooker beginning on the day before the battle. Describing Hooker, he reported, "He had to the full that joy of battle which McClellan never had at all: and showed it." Smalley's graphic report of the next day's bloody events scooped every other paper in the country and he gave his readers hard facts, as opposed to the vague generalities usually offered up. He filed the first installment of his report from Frederick, Maryland, at about 7:00 a.m. on September 18, from a telegraph office that had been commandeered by the War Office. His report was relayed directly to Secretary Edwin M. Stanton before being passed to New York, and it was the first full account of the events that President Lincoln saw and read to his cabinet. Deciding to send a more complete report of the battle from Baltimore by telegraph, Smiley arrived in Baltimore just as the express train to New York was about to leave the station and decided to hop on. Positioning himself under an oil lamp in the New York train, he began to write his opener: "Fierce and desperate battle between 200,000 men has raged since daylight, yet night closes on an uncertain field. It is the greatest fight since Waterloo—all over the field contested with an obstinacy equal even to Waterloo." When he arrived at 6:00 a.m., the *Tribune's* typesetting and printing crew went to work. Two hours later, the story, considered the best piece of journalism to come out of the Civil War, hit the streets.

troops who had survived five major Union attacks the day before, who could still fight, and who expected to on the morning of September 18. So did McClellan, who wired General Henry Halleck in Washington at 8:00 a.m.: "The battle will probably be renewed today. Send all the troops you can by the most expeditious route." During the day McClellan received 13,000 reinforcements, added to the 20,000 fresh troops he had held in reserve the previous day, which was more than Lee had remaining in his entire army. But McClellan delayed again, continuing to operate under the impression that Lee's army still outnumbered his and convincing himself there was no assurance of his success if he renewed the fight. In his official report, written a year later, he stated: "I concluded that the success of an attack on the 18th was not certain. . . . I should have had a narrow view of the condition of the country had I been willing to hazard another battle with less than an absolute assurance of success."

So, on September 18, while occasional gunfire could be heard as teams began sorting through the bodies and horrendous evidence of the single bloodiest day of battle, General Lee concluded that afternoon that the campaign in the north was lost and made his plans to retreat after dark. Around midnight the Army of Northern Virginia began its escape across the Potomac at Boteler's Ford. Through the night and into the morning, Lee's men crossed into Virginia unopposed.

Casualties

The long process of attending to wounded and sick soldiers, burying the dead, and clearing up the general destruction in the wake of the Battle of Antietam began the minute the guns fell silent. Eyewitness accounts of the evening of September 17 tell of the terrible cries in the night of the great number of wounded and the dying that had to be left on the battlefield until spare hands could be found to attend to them. A lucky few were searched for by their fellow soldiers and the experiences of those who searched, stumbling over so much devastation, are horrifying.

The entire area became "one vast hospital," a local reporter wrote, and a burial ground, with

"Detained in superintending the removal of a number of the wounded of my division, I was among the last to cross the Potomac. As I rode into the river I passed General Lee, sitting on his horse in the stream, watching the crossing of the wagons and artillery. Returning my greeting, he inquired as to what was still behind. There was nothing but the wagons containing my wounded, and a battery of artillery, all of which were near at hand, and I told him so. 'Thank God!' I heard him say as I rode on."
—**Confederate Brigadier General John George Walker.**

Antietam

Burial crews at the Bloody Lane.

local people, not only from Sharpsburg but towns all around the area, taking care of the estimated 17,000 wounded soldiers from both sides in their homes or helping in makeshift hospitals established in any space available. Field hospitals in tents with beds of straw for the patients were placed in the fields by the military and manned by government personnel and volunteers that came from as far away as Washington, Baltimore, and beyond. Among the volunteers was Clara Barton, perhaps the most famous civilian volunteer of the war, who arrived during the battle with a wagonload of medical supplies. The Dunker Church, although badly damaged by shellfire, was among the buildings left standing on the battlefield that was used as a hospital. Employing a system introduced by Dr. Jonathan Letterman, chief medical officer of the Union Army of the Potomac, who used the Pry

Clara Barton.

Burial crew with a single grave on the battlefield.

Smith's barn used as a hospital.

House as his headquarters, an ambulance corps to evacuate wounded, a triage system of prioritizing care, and the field hospitals were all set in place.

The day after the battle and for many days that followed, the families and friends of soldiers began to arrive in Sharpsburg to look for sons, husbands, and fathers, having heard news of the terrible battle that had taken place there. Some of the lucky ones, strong enough to be moved, were taken home to recover by family members. Among those that came was Dr. Oliver Wendell Holmes, whose son

In every direction around men were digging graves and burying the dead. Ten or twelve bodies lay at the different pits and had already become offensive. In front of this wood was the bloody cornfield where lay two or three hundred festering bodies, nearly all of Rebels, the most hideous exhibition I had yet seen. Many were black as Negroes, heads and faces hideously swelled, covered with dust. . . . From among these loathsome earth-soiled vestiges of humanity, the soldiers were still picking out some that had life left and carrying them in on stretchers to our surgeons. . . . In the midst of all this carrion our troops sat cooking, eating, jabbering, and smoking; sleeping among the corpses so that but for the color of the skin it was difficult to distinguish the living from the dead.

—From the diary of Union Colonel David Hunter Strother, September 18, 1862.

Burying the dead.

was wounded in the West Woods. Having searched one field hospital after another, he finally spotted his son on a train that was about to move the wounded north from the Hagerstown station.

Typhoid and cholera rapidly became a threat because of the heat and the massive number of decaying dead bodies that proved to be a challenge for those unlucky enough to do the work of burying them. Forty-two percent of the Antietam dead could not be identified because dog tags were not yet issued by the military, although some soldiers wore some sort of identification that they supplied themselves. Union soldiers generally identified their own dead when that was possible, but Confederate soldiers were not so lucky. Bodies were buried singularly or in mass graves, anywhere a burial spot could be found and in many cases with little care or

Field hospital near Keedysville, Maryland.

ceremony. Military details, with the help of locals, some paid to do the dreadful job, got the task done, marking the thousands of graves with less than permanent markers. Burying so many dead took days.

By March 1864 many of the shallow graves had become exposed. Later that year a plan was initiated to create a permanent burial place for these soldiers. On the fifth anniversary of the battle, President Andrew Johnson and other dignitaries officially dedicated the Antietam National Cemetery, today under the care of the National Park Service, as a place of remembrance.

In early December each year, local volunteers remember the Antietam dead in another way. Thousands of candles are placed on the battlefield—one candle representing every Union or Confederate soldier killed, wounded, or missing

Confederate bodies gathered for burial.

on September 17, 1862. After dark, at about 6:00 p.m., visitors are invited to drive through the park to view the moving illumination of the battlefield. The Antietam National Battlefield Memorial Illumination ceremony takes place on the first Saturday in December annually.

Union soldier's grave; a Confederate body awaits burial.

The Days That Followed

Not until September 20, 1862, did McClellan pursue Lee, sending a few Fifth Corps regiments that A. P. Hill's men repelled. Two days later, Lincoln issued his Emancipation Proclamation, declaring that if the Confederate states did not return to the Union by January 1, 1863, their slaves "shall be then, thenceforward, and forever free." From October 1 to October 4, President Lincoln went to Antietam to visit McClellan and his troops and to urge the general to actively pursue the Confederate army. Totally frustrated by McClellan, Lincoln relieved him of his command on November 7, 1862, due to what the president said was a

Lincoln with McClellan's officers at Sharpsburg, October 1862.

Antietam

Ozias M. Hatch, who accompanied President Lincoln to Sharpsburg when he met with McClellan, wrote:

> *Lincoln said to me, "Come, Hatch, I want you to take a walk with me.". . . He led me about the camp, and then we walked upon the surrounding hills overlooking the great city of white tents and sleeping soldiers. . . . Finally, reaching a commanding point where almost that entire camp could be seen—the men were just beginning their morning duties, and evidences of life and activity were becoming apparent—we involuntarily stopped.*
>
> *The President, waving his hand towards the scene before us, and leaning towards me, said in an almost whispering voice: "Hatch, Hatch, what is all this?" "Why, Mr. Lincoln," said I, "this is the Army of the Potomac." He hesitated a moment, and then, straightening up, said in a louder tone. "No, Hatch, no. This is General McClellan's body-guard."*

"bad case of the slows." The war would continue for one and a half more years, but it was left to another general to finally defeat General Lee and reunite the nation.

Antietam: A Tourist's Guide to Exploring, Staying, and Eating

PLACES TO VISIT NEARBY

Antietam National Cemetery, 5831 Dunker Church Road, Sharpsburg, Md., (301) 432-5124, www.nps.gov/anti. The burial place of Union soldiers who died at the battles of Antietam, Moncracy, South Mountain, and other engagements, the eleven-acre cemetery was established in March 1865. At the center of the cemetery is a statue of a Union soldier facing homeward to commemorate the dead.

Antietam National Cemetery.

National Cemetery, Antietam Battlefield, Md.

Grove Farm Marker, Shepherdstown Pike (Highway 34, on the left when traveling east), Sharpsburg, Md., www.hmdb.org/marker .asp?marker=1969. The farm of Stephen P. Grove was a Union camp during the Battle of Antietam and the house on the property was the head-quarters for General Fitz-John Porter and his Fifth Corps. In early October 1862 Lincoln met with General McClellan at Sharpsburg and came to the farm to review the Fifth Corps. Alexander Gardner's famous photos of Lincoln meeting with McClellan are posed in front of the Grove house, which still stands.

Heart of the Civil War Heritage Area. Sharpsburg and the Antietam battlefield are only a few of many Civil War sites to visit in the area. Known locally as the Civil War Heritage Area, Washington, Frederick, and Carroll Counties form the heart of it. The state of Maryland Heritage Areas Authority have set up a useful Web site that offers plenty of information for tourists interested in local Civil War history: www .HeartOfTheCivilWar.org. Or you can phone them at (800) 999-3613.

The Kennedy Farmhouse, 2406 Chestnut Grove Road, Sharpsburg, Md., (202) 537-8900, www .johnbrown.org. Abolitionist John Brown (using the name Isaac Smith) and his sons Owen and Oliver rented this house for $35 in Sharpsburg, where they planned their October 1859 raid on the arse-nal at Harpers Ferry, just 6 miles away. Tours of the house can be arranged by appointment for a fee; (202) 537-8900, www.johnbrown.org.

John Brown.

Lee Headquarters Marker, Shepherdstown Pike (Highway 34, on the right when traveling east), Sharpsburg, Md., www.hmdb.org/marker.asp?marker=5640. The Robert E. Lee Memorial Tablet marks the location of General Lee's head-quarters in the Oak Grove from September 15 to September 18, 1862.

Pry House Field Hospital Museum, Shepherds-town Pike (Highway 34), Keedysville, Md., (301) 416-2395. Open 11–5 daily June to October, and on weekends only in May and November. Call the museum to confirm visiting hours. A $2 donation is suggested. Sponsored by the National Museum of Civil War Medicine, this museum is located in the house on the grounds of the Pry farm that General

Pry Farm.

George McClellan used as his headquarters and from which he observed the Battle of Antietam on September 17, 1862. It was used also as the medical headquarters for Dr. Jonathan Letterman, who planned the field medicine system used to care for Antietam's wounded. Exhibits and interpretive panels offer Pry House history, re-create an operating theater, display objects used to care for patients, and tell the grim story of how survivors of the battle were cared for and what impact this had on civilians who lived in the area.

HOTELS

There are only a few places in which to find a bed for the night in Sharpsburg. These and a selection of other smaller, privately run operations within a reasonable driving distance to the battlefield are listed below. You will find your favorite chains of motels in Hagerstown, Maryland (16 miles to the north), and Frederick, Maryland (about 22 miles to the east), by checking the chains' Web sites.

An old postcard shot of Main Street in Sharpsburg.

Bavarian Inn.

Bavarian Inn, 164 Shepherd Grade Road, Shepherdstown, W.V., (304) 876-2551, www.bavarian innwv.com. Its position above the Potomac River offers commanding views from some of the seventy-three comfortable rooms in the chalets spread on this property. Located about 4 miles from the Antietam battlefield and with an excellent restaurant (see Restaurants), it's a great base from which to visit the many Civil War sites in the area.

The Inn at Antietam Bed and Breakfast, 220 East Main Street, Sharpsburg, Md., (301) 432-6601, www.innatantietam.com. This Victorian mansion, with a wraparound porch and a view of the Blue Ridge Mountains from the patio and garden, is located in the center of Sharpsburg. Five comfortable suites accommodate guests.

Jacob Rohrbach Inn, 138 West Main Street, Sharpsburg, Md., (301) 432-5079, www.jacob-rohrbach-inn.com. Furnished with antiques, this nineteenth-century house has been turned into a comfortable hotel with modern amenities. If you want to walk to the Antietam battlefield, this is the place to stay. It offers five rooms.

Stone Manor Vineyard and Orchard Bed and Breakfast, 13193 Mountain Road, Lovettsville, Va., (540) 822-5409, www.mycountryretreat.com. Located on a country road below South Mountain in a hundred-year-old stone house, the manor is about 25 miles from Sharpsburg and close to many other Civil War sites. Virginia's Loudon Wine Trail is also nearby. Comfortable beds, large and interesting rooms, and Beth and Spencer's excellent breakfasts, handmade soaps, and abundance of hospitality make it very tough to get inspired to go out and see the local sites.

Stone Manor.

Thomas Shepherd Inn, corner of Duke and German Streets, Shepherdstown, W.V., (888) 889-8952, www.thomasshepherdinn.com. The inn is located only 4 miles from Sharpsburg, in the bustling town of Shepherdstown, which was overwhelmed by casualties of the battle fought nearby in 1862. It's the only B&B in town and has six homey, well-appointed rooms.

RESTAURANTS

Bavarian Inn, 164 Shepherd Grade Road, Shepherdstown, W.V., (304) 876-2551, www.bavarian innwv.com. With an elegant, old-world dining room, extensive menu that includes many German specialties, and a selection of seasonal game dishes, this is a comfortable place to unwind and replenish after a long day touring the Antietam battlefield.

Bavarian Inn's comfortable dining room.

Captain Benders Tavern, 111 East Main Street, Sharpsburg, Md., (301) 432-5812, www.captain benders.com. Billing themselves as "the most successful tavern in South Washington County," this is one of the few places where you can find a meal or a drink in Sharpsburg. It's a friendly local spot with a full range of appetizers (nachos, wings, egg rolls) and a good selection of salads, burgers, and other sandwiches. No breakfast and no lunch on Monday.

Grandale Farm Restaurant, 13997 Harpers Ferry Road, Purcellville, Va., (540) 668-6000, www .grandalefarm.com. Across the Potomac, about 22 miles from Sharpsburg, this simple but cozy dining room (in winter there's a roaring fire) overlooks the fruit trees on the farm. Farm-fresh produce and local products are featured on the menu, along with a selection of Loudon County wines. No breakfast.

Magnolias at the Mill, 198 North 21st Street, Purcellville, Va., (540) 338-9800, www.purcellville restaurant.com. Magnolias' warm and attractive atmosphere in a 1905 mill building, located in the center of town, makes it a fun place to eat and drink, as does its interesting menu. Soups and salads, burgers, steaks, and fish entrees are visually enticing as well as satisfying after a long day visiting Antietam. Excellent food is served here with lots of Southern touches. No breakfast.

Glossary

artillery: Large-caliber guns; also the unit of the military that uses those guns.

battery: Unit of the military consisting of guns, men, and vehicles to transport the guns.

bayonet: A sharp blade, fixed onto a muzzle of a rifle, used for stabbing in hand-to-hand fighting.

brigade: A military unit made up of five regiments or battalions. During the Civil War a brigade usually contained about 3,000 soldiers and was led by a brigadier general.

canister: A metal container filled usually with iron balls or other metal objects and sawdust, inserted in a large-caliber gun, and used generally against infantry at close range.

cavalry: Military units that fought on horseback during the Civil War. In modern warfare, cavalry fight in tanks.

corps: A large military force commanded by a major general. The U.S. Army of the Potomac had six corps, each with 10,000 to 15,000 soldiers. The Confederate Army's corps were larger, containing about 20,000 soldiers.

division: A military unit made up of several brigades, each usually containing about 3,000 soldiers, led by a lieutenant general.

dog tags: Metal identity tags the military wear around their necks.

earthworks: A large bank of soil used for defensive purposes.

flank: The right or left side of an army; to flank is to attack from the side or rake with gunfire.

infantry: Soldiers who fight on foot.

marksman: One skilled at shooting with a pistol or rifle.

outflank: To move around the side of the enemy with the purpose of outmaneuvering them.

secede: Withdraw from membership.

shock troops: A group of soldiers trained to carry out sudden assault.

triage: Assignment of degrees of urgency of treatment when many people are wounded or ill.

Zouaves: Civil War units modeled after French infantry, originally recruited from the mountains of Algeria, who demonstrated a particular hardiness and bravery in battle. The American Zouaves modeled their colorful uniforms after those of the French troops: red baggy trousers, a short jacket, large sash, and a fez or turban worn instead of a cap.

Bibliography

Bradford, James C., editor. *Atlas of American Military History.* New York: Oxford University Press, 2003.

Commager, Henry S., editor. *The Blue and the Gray.* New York: Bobbs-Merrill Company, Inc., 1950.

Ernst, Kathleen A. *Too Afraid to Cry: Maryland Civilians in the Antietam Campaign.* Mechanicsburg, Pa.: Stackpole Books, 2007.

Ethier, Eric, and Rebecca Aloisi. *Insiders' Guide to Civil War Sites in the Eastern Theater,* 3rd edition. Guilford, Conn.: Globe Pequot Press, 2008.

Evans, Clement A., editor. *Confederate Military History.* Atlanta, Ga.: Confederate Publishing Company, 1899.

Frassanito, William A. *Antietam: The Photographic Legacy of America's Bloodiest Day.* New York: Charles Scribner's Sons, 1978.

Freeman, D. S. *R. E. Lee,* Vol. II. New York: Charles Scribner's Sons, 1934.

Hassler, Warren W., Jr. *General George B. McClellan, Shield of the Union.* Baton Rouge, La.: Louisiana State University Press, 1957.

Henderson, G. F. R. *Stonewall Jackson and the American Civil War.* London: Longmans, Green and Company, 1955.

Hitchcock, Frederick L. *War from the Inside: The Story of the 132nd Regiment Pennsylvania Volunteer Infantry in the War for the Suppression of the Rebellion.* Philadelphia: J. B. Lippincott, 1904.

Johnson, Clifton. *Battleground Adventures.* Boston
and New York: Houghton Mifflin Company,
1915.

Longstreet, James. *From Manassas to Appomattox.* Philadelphia: J. B. Lippincott and Company,
1896.

McPherson, James M. *Crossroads of Freedom:
Antietam.* New York: Oxford University Press,
2002.

Moore, Frank. *Anecdotes, Poetry, and Incidents of
the War.* New York: The Arundel Print, 1882.

Sears, Stephen W. *Landscape Turned Red: The
Battle of Antietam.* New York: Ticknor & Fields,
1983.

Bibliography

Index

Antietam

Index